D0124593

JUSTIN's CHUCKLE TIME

JUSTIN FLETCHER

Illustrated by Patrick Tate

faber and faber

C0000 002 647 468

First published in 2013
by Faber and Faber Limited
Bloomsbury House
74-77 Great Russell Street
London WC1B 3DA

Designed by Patrick Tate
Printed in England by CPI Group (UK) Ltd, Croydon CRO 4YY

All rights reserved

Collection © Justin Fletcher, 2013
Illustrations © Patrick Tate, 2013

The right of Justin Fletcher to be identified as author of this
work has been asserted in accordance with Section 77 of
the Copyright, Designs and Patents Act 1988

This book is sold subject to the condition that it shall not,
by way of trade or otherwise, be lent, resold, hired out or
otherwise circulated without the publisher's prior consent
in any form of binding or cover other than that in which
it is published and without a similar condition including this
condition being imposed on the subsequent purchaser

A CIP record for this book is available from the British
Library

978-0571-30353-3

FSC
www.fsc.org
MIX
Paper from
responsible sources
FSC® C101712

2 4 6 8 10 9 7 5 3 1

Hello, boys and girls.

Do you like jokes? I do – the sillier, the better!

  I've put all my favourite and funniest jokes in this book, just for you. Some jokes will make you giggle – and others will make you groan . . .

  Hope you have lots of lovely laughs!

Love,

JuSTiN X

Animal Antics

My dog, Engelbert, is always doing silly things. He really makes me laugh - just like these crazy creatures!

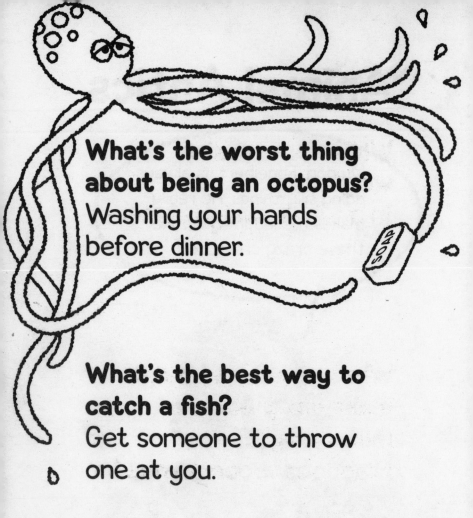

What's the worst thing about being an octopus?
Washing your hands before dinner.

What's the best way to catch a fish?
Get someone to throw one at you.

Where are whales weighed?
In a whale-weigh station.

What noise does a cat make going down a motorway?
Miaooooooooooooowww!

Which dog likes having bubble baths?
A shampoodle.

What do you call a sheep with no legs?
A cloud.

What is a frog's favourite sweet?
A lollihop.

What's the biggest mouse in the world?
A hippopotamouse.

What do you call a cow eating grass?
A lawnmooer.

What animal can you eat for pudding?
A moose.

Which lion never roars?
A dandelion.

GRRR!

Why can leopards never escape from the zoo?
Because they're always spotted.

Why should you never play card games in the jungle?
Because there are so many cheetahs around.

☆ ☆ ☆ ☆ ☆ ☆ ☆

Ask Justin!

Justin, what's your
favourite animal?

My dog Engelbert is
my best friend!

What do you call a
monkey with a banana
in each ear?
Anything you like - it
can't hear you.

Where can you always
find a cow?
In a moo-seum.

**What do hedgehogs say
when they kiss?**
'Ouch!'

**What do you call a donkey
with three legs?**
A wonkey.

What do you
call a donkey
with one eye
and three legs?
A winkey wonkey.

When is it bad luck to
meet a black cat?
When you're a mouse.

Why did the owl 'owl?
Because the woodpecker
woodpecker.

**How can you tell which
end of a worm is its
head?**
Tickle his middle and see
which end smiles.

What do cats like to eat on a hot day?

A mice cream cone.

Jumbo Jokes

What should you do if an elephant sneezes?
Get out of the way.

**Can an elephant jump
higher than a lamp post?**
Yes. Lamp posts can't
jump, silly!

**Why are elephants
covered in wrinkles?**
Well, have you ever tried
to iron an elephant?

Ask Justin!

What is your favourite colour?

Yellow is my favourite colour - like sunshine!

What time is it when an elephant sits on your car?
Time to get a new car.

What's the difference between a biscuit and an elephant?
You can't dip an elephant into your tea.

How does an elephant get down from a tree?
He sits on a leaf and
waits for autumn.

What's grey and red all over?
An embarrassed elephant.

What do you give an elephant with big feet?
Plenty of room.

Why do elephants paint their toenails red?
So they can hide in cherry trees.

Have you ever seen an
elephant in a cherry tree?
No.
Shows how well it works!

What do you get if you cross a jellyfish with an elephant?
Jelly the elephant.

24

Fairy Tale Fun

You've never seen your favourite characters like this before! Hee hee!

What kind of pet does Aladdin have?
A car-pet.

Who has green hair and eats porridge?
Mouldilocks.

Why was Cinderella a terrible football player?
She had a pumpkin for a coach.

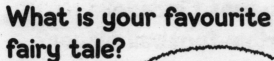

Ask Justin!

What is your favourite fairy tale?

I like Snow White because the Seven Dwarves make me laugh!

Who flies through the air in his underwear?
Peter Pants.

29

Do mermaids use knives and forks when they eat? No, they use their fish fingers.

**What do you call a giant
in a phone box?**
Stuck.

**What do you call a wicked
old lady who lives by the
sea?**
A sandwitch.

What do witches race each other on?
Vroomsticks.

Where do ghosts live?
In dead ends.

Food Funnies

Yum! These terrifically tasty jokes are making me feel hungry!

33

What do pixies have for tea?
Fairy cakes.

What's white, fluffy and swings through the trees?
A meringue-utang.

**How do you
make a milk shake?**
Jump out and
give it a scare!

BOO!!!

**What starts with 'T', end
in 'T' and is full of 'T'?**
A teapot.

Why was the strawberry sad?
Because it was in a jam.

What's the best thing to put into a pie?
Your teeth.

What kind of pie can fly?
A magpie.

What kind of nut hangs on the wall?
A walnut.

What is the fastest vegetable?
A runner bean.

go bean !

What's the strongest vegetable?
A muscle sprout.

Which letter is a vegetable?
A 'P'.

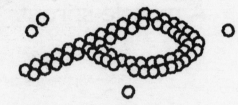

What's yellow on the inside and green on the outside?
A banana disguised as a cucumber.

Ask Justin!

What is your favourite fruit?

I don't know how to choose! I love apples and oranges and bananas too.

41

What's tall, stands in the middle of Paris and wobbles? The Trifle Tower.

What do you call two bananas on the floor?
A pair of slippers.

Why are bananas never lonely?
Because they hang around in bunches.

**What did the skeleton
order for dinner?**
Spare ribs.

**What's worse than finding
a worm in your apple?**
Finding half a worm in
your apple.

What vegetable shouldn't be served on a ship?
A leek.

Which day of the week do potatoes hate?
Fry-day.

What is a gorilla's favourite snack?

A chocolate chimp cookie.

Cluck, cluck!

Why did the chicken cross the road?
To get to the other side.

Why did the chicken run across the road?
Because he wanted to get to the other side faster.

Why did the chicken cross the playground?
To get to the other slide.

**Why did the chicken cross
the beach?**
To get to the other tide.

**Why did the duck cross
the road?**
Because it was the
chicken's day off.

Why did the chicken cross the road again?
Because it needed the eggs-ercise.

Why did the fox cross the road?
It was chasing the chicken.

Ask Justin!

What do you want for your birthday?

I always like a birthday cake with candles to blow out!

Why did the chicken stop crossing the road?
Because it was tired of all the chicken jokes!

On which side does a chicken have most feathers?
On the outside.

What did the chicken say when it laid a square egg?
'Ouch!'

Why do chickens lay eggs?
Because if they dropped them, they'd break.

Knock, knock

Who's there?

Arthur.

Arthur who?

Arthur any more biscuits?

Knock, knock.

Who's there?

Luke.

Luke who?

Luke through the letterbox and you'll see.

Knock, knock.

Who's there?

Flea.

Flea who?

Flea's a jolly good fellow . . .

Knock, knock.

Who's there?

Major.

Major who?

Major open the door!

Ask Justin!

What do you like to eat for breakfast?

I love to have pancakes as a special treat!

Knock, knock.

Who's there?

Doughnut.

Doughnut who?

Doughnut ask - it's a secret.

Knock, knock.

Who's there?

Lego.

Lego who?

Lego of me and I'll tell you!

62

Knock, knock.

Who's there?

Hairy.

Hairy who?

Hairy up and

let me in.

Knock, knock.

Who's there?

Kanga.

Kanga who?

No, kanga*roo*.

Knock, knock.

Who's there?

William.

William who?

Williamind your own business!

Knock, knock.

Who's there?

Hugo.

Hugo who?

**Hugo that way and
I'll go this way.**

Knock, knock.

Who's there?

Bean.

Bean who?

Bean a while since I last saw you.

Knock, knock.

Who's there?

Radio.

Radio who?

Radio not, here I come!

Knock, knock.

Who's there?

Police.

Police who?

Police can I come in?

Knock, knock.

Who's there?

Cowsgo.

Cowsgo who?

Cows go moo, silly!

MOOOOO!

Silly Creepy Crawlies

Bugs are brilliant - and these bug jokes are 'un-bee-lievable'!

**Why were flies playing
football in the saucer?**
They were playing for
the cup!

**What do you say to an
annoying insect?**
'Stop bugging me!'

How do you start an insect race?

'One, two, flea, go!'

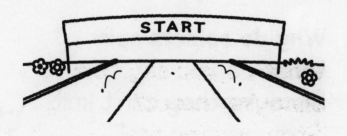

Why did the fly fly?
Because the spider
spied 'er.

**Why do spiders spin
webs?**
Because they can't knit.

**What did one firefly say
to the other?**
'Got to glow now!'

**What's the biggest kind
of moth?**
A mam-moth.

What goes 'Hum-choo!
Hum-choo!'?
A bee with a cold.

What did the mummy bee
say to the naughty bee?
'Beehive yourself!'

Why do bees hum?
Because they always forget the words.

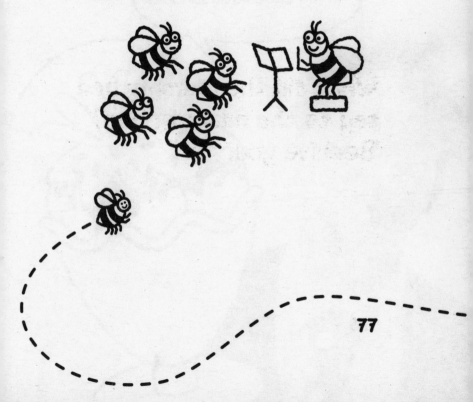

What did the bee say to the flower?
'Hello, honey!'

What's the biggest ant in the world?
An eleph-ant.

Why was the baby ant confused?
Because all her uncles were ants.

What is even smaller than an ant's dinner?
An ant's mouth.

Why don't centipedes play football?
It takes them too long to put on their boots.

**What did the
earwig say
when it fell
down the
stairs?**
'Ear we go!'

**Why is the letter 'T' so
important to a stick
insect?**
Without it, it would be a
sick insect.

Christmas Crackers

There's 'snow' joke like a Christmas joke!

Why is it cold at Christmas time?
Because it's in Decembrrrrr . . .

What do ducks love about Christmas?
Pulling the Christmas quackers.

How do snowmen get around?
By icicle.

**Where do snowmen
go dancing?**
At a snowball.

**Why did the dog stay
up on Christmas Eve?**
He wanted to see
Santa Paws.

Ask Justin!

What do you like best about Christmas?

I love singing carols!

Christmas Carols

What goes 'Now you see me, now you don't, now you see me, now you don't.'?
A snowman on a zebra crossing.

What do skunks sing at Christmas time?
'Jingle smells, jingle smells . . .'

Who is Father Christmas married to?
Mary Christmas.

What do mice write on their Christmas cards?
Happy Chris-mouse!

**What's red and white and
red and white?**
Santa rolling down a hill.

**Which of Santa's reindeer
has bad manners?**
Rude-olph.

What do reindeer hang on their Christmas trees?
Hornaments.

**What do reindeer have
that no other animals
have?**
Baby reindeer.

Do reindeer go to school?
No, they're elf-taught.

How do you scare a snowman?

Get a hair dryer.

Doctor, Doctor!

Doctor, Doctor, I feel like a pair of curtains!
Well, pull yourself together then.

Doctor, Doctor, I feel like a spoon.
Sit down and don't stir.

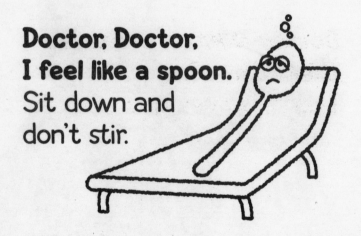

**Doctor, Doctor, I keep
thinking I'm invisible.**
Who said that?

**Doctor, Doctor, everyone
thinks I'm a liar.**
I don't believe you.

Doctor, Doctor, everyone keeps being rude to me.
Get out of here, you silly thing.

Doctor, Doctor, I keep thinking I'm a dog.
Well, sit down and tell me all about it.
I can't I'm not allowed on the furniture.

Doctor, Doctor, I keep thinking I'm a strawberry. You're really in a jam, aren't you?

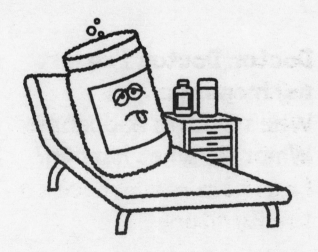

Doctor, Doctor, I keep thinking I'm a dustbin.
Don't talk rubbish.

Doctor, Doctor, I've lost my memory.
When did this happen?
When did what happen?

Doctor, Doctor, I keep thinking I'm a goat.
How long have you felt like this for?
Since I was a kid.

Ask Justin!

Which do you prefer - a picnic in the park or on the beach?

My dog Engelbert and I love the beach!

Doctor, Doctor, everyone keeps ignoring me.
Next please!

Doctor, Doctor, I've just swallowed my pen. What shall I do?
Use a pencil!

Doctor, Doctor, I keep thinking I'm a bridge!
What's come over you?
Three cars, a lorry and a motorbike.

Why did the light bulb visit the doctor?
It kept having hot flashes.

Potty Pirates

Ahaarr, me hearties!
All hands on deck
and 'jokes ahoy'!

Why don't pirates get hungry on desert islands?
Because of all the sand which is there.

Why didn't the pirate say 'Aye, aye, Captain'?
Because his Captain has only one eye.

How do pirates get from ship to ship?
By taxi crab.

What do you get if you cross a pie and a rat?
A pie-rat!

What's a pirate's favourite pudding?
Jelly Roger.

What has five eyes, ten ears and five legs?
Five pirates.

**How does
Captain Hook
scratch his
nose?**
Very carefully!

**What is a pirate's
favourite letter of the
alphabet?**
All pirates love the 'C'.

**When is the best time
for a pirate to buy a new
ship?**
When it's on sail.

**Why couldn't the pirates
play cards?**
The Captain was standing
on the deck.

What is a pirate's favourite dance? The Hokey Cokey - because you put one leg in and one leg out!

**How much did
the pirate's
earrings cost?**
A buccaneer.

**What do you get when
you cross a parrot and
a shark?**
A bird that talks your
ear off.

What happens if a big hairy monster sits in front of you at the cinema?
You miss most of the movie.

What is a vampire's favourite dance?
The fang-dango.

How do you greet a monster with three heads?

'Hello, hello, hello.'

What should you do if a monster runs in the front door?
Run out of the back door.

What is a monster's favourite bean?
A human bean.

Why did the monster eat a light bulb?
He wanted a light snack.

119

Did you hear about the monster who had eight arms?
He said they came in handy.

Who is the cleverest monster?
Frank-Einstein.

What's the difference between a big, hairy monster and an ice cream?
Kids like ice creams.

YUK!

What has a purple spotty body, ten legs and big eyes on stalks?
I don't know but there's one crawling up your arm!

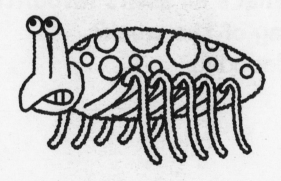

**What would you do if
a one-legged monster
knocked at your door?**
Tell him to hop it.

**What's an alien's favourite
day of the week?**
Moonday.

What do aliens like to eat?
Mars-malade.

Where do aliens park their spaceships?
At parking meteors.

What is an alien's favourite board game?
Moonopoly.

Where do ogres go on holiday?
Aus-troll-ia.

How does the yeti feel when he's sick?
Abominable.

What does a monster eat in a restaurant?
The waiter.

help!

Waiter, waiter, there's a
fly in my soup.
Don't worry, sir, the spider
in the salad will get it.

Waiter, waiter, there's a
fly in my soup.
Don't worry, sir, they
don't eat much.

Waiter, waiter, what's this fly doing in my soup?
I think it's doing the backstroke, sir.

**Waiter, waiter, there's a
fly in my soup.**
Please don't shout, sir, or
the other customers will
want one too.

**Waiter, waiter, there's a
frog in my soup.**
Yes, sir, the fly's gone on
holiday.

Waiter, waiter, there's a caterpillar in my salad.
Don't worry, madam, there's no extra charge.

**Waiter, waiter, do you
serve crabs?**
Sit down, sir, we serve
anybody.

Waiter, waiter, have you got frog's legs?
No, madam, I always walk like this.

Waiter, waiter, there's something wrong with my eggs.
Don't ask me, sir, I only laid the table.

Waiter, waiter, there's a small slug in my salad.
I'm sorry, sir, would you like me to get you a bigger one?

Waiter, waiter, there's a fly in the butter.
Yes, madam, it's a butterfly.

Justin's Mad Mix-up

Welcome to my crazy collection of jokes about anything and everything!

What's yellow, brown and hairy?
Cheese and toast on the carpet.

What do you call two banana peels?
A pair of slippers.

Which room has no door, ceiling or windows?
A mushroom.

What do you call an igloo without a toilet?
An ig.

Shall I tell you the joke about the pencil?
No, there's no point in it.

Shall I tell you the joke about the bed?
No, it hasn't been made yet.

What do you call a fish with no eyes?
A fsh.

What do you call a reluctant bird?
A pelican't.

Which keys are furry?
Monkeys.

**What do you call a
disappearing aeroplane?**
Boeing, going, gone.

What kind of bow is impossible to tie?
A rainbow.

Why did the apple cry?
Its peelings were hurt.

**Which pets make the
most noise?**
Trumpets.

**Where do
you learn
to make
ice cream?**
Sundae school.

9/10

How should you dress on a cold day?
Really quickly!

What disappears every time you stand up?
Your lap.

What sort of mistakes do ghosts make?
Boo-boos.

What does a house wear?
Address.

How do you start a jelly race?

'Ready, set, go!'

What is a volcano?
A mountain with hiccups!

hic!

**What's the last thing
you take off before you
go to bed?**
Your feet off the floor.

**Why are pianos hard
to open?**
The keys are inside.

**What
do ghosts
send home
from their
holidays?**
Ghost-cards.

**What do you call a
dinosaur who never
gives up?**
A try-try-triceratops.

Why did the golfer bring two pairs of pants to the game?
In case he got a hole in one.

What colour is a hiccup?
Burple!

Did you enjoy all my jokes? I hope you had a 'giggletastic' time!

Why don't you tell some of your favourite jokes to your friends and see if they like them too?

Goodbye for now - and keep on laughing!

Love,

JuSTiN X

Also available: